BIDDESDEN COOKERY

BIDDESDEN COOKERY

MIRABEL GUINNESS

illustrated by
ROLAND PYM

MOUNT ORLEANS PRESS

METRIC CONVERSIONS
approximate

1 oz	30 g
⅓ lb	150 g
½ lb	225 g
1 lb	450 g
½ pint	0.25 l
1 pint	0.5 l
200° F	100° C
350° F	180° C
430° F	220° C

First published
in 1987 by Anthony Eyre
Chiseldon, Wiltshire

This edition published 2019 by
Mount Orleans Press
23 High Street, Cricklade, SN6 6AP
https://anthonyeyre.com

ISBN 978 1 912945 03 0

All rights reserved
Text © Mirabel Helme
Illustrations © the Estate of Roland Pym

Printed in Italy
by L.E.G.O. S.p.A.
Lavis (TN)

To Alice

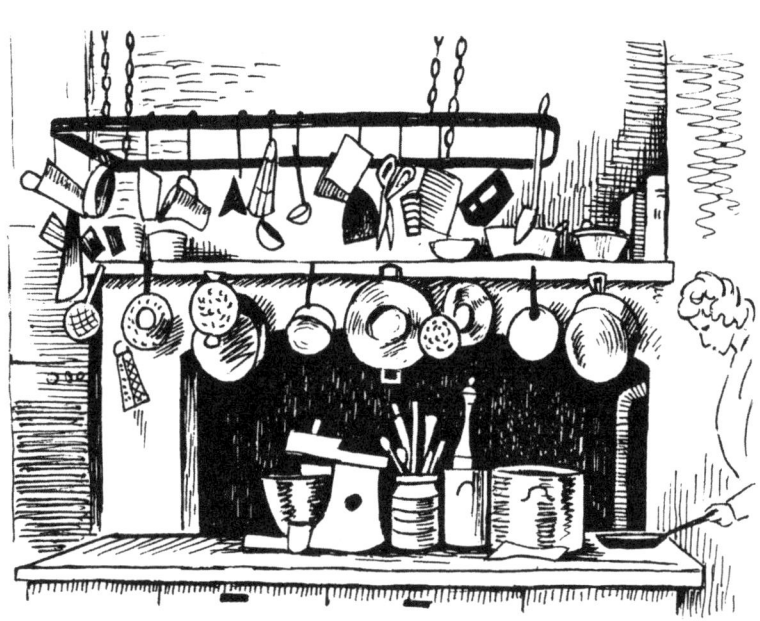

Contents

Introduction	9
Soups	15
Starters	21
Sauces	31
Vegetables	39
Main Courses	47
Puddings	59
Cakes	77
Drinks	89
Index	95

Introduction

Biddesden House was built in 1710 for General Webb, one of Marlborough's generals famous for his military victory at Wynendael. It is built of brick of two colours, pinkish red and slatey blue which from a distance give a soft effect. The façade has a neat symmetry with three round windows over the front door and the General's trophies standing up on the roof against the sky. On the east side of the house is a tower (*page 51*), built to hold the bell which was presented to General Webb by the grateful citizens of Lille after he relieved the siege there.

Biddesden is the grand house it was intended to be, but not too grand. Despite the tower and the trophies, it is not too ostentatious and everything seems to have its purpose; even the vast portrait by Wootton of the General on horseback which dominates the front hall is essential. The General's ghost galloped noisily up and down the stairs when a previous owner went off with the picture, which then had to be bought back to silence the thundering hooves.

My father came to live at Biddesden in 1931. He married my mother in 1936, they had nine children and I am the youngest. My mother was brought up in Argyll and my father spent his childhood in Ireland and London, yet after little over a half a century of being there their family seems to have become deeply rooted in Wiltshire. Biddesden has changed very little since the 1930s. The dining room is as it was with its large lilac-grey table surrounded by high-backed chairs and the massive elaborately carved side table. It has a black and white marble top on which dish after dish have rested after their progression along the passage from the kitchen. The kitchen used to have a great black coal-burning range with compartments above it for keeping plates warm. It still has a huge scrubbed oak table with enormous drawers for holding wooden spoons and a large assortment of cake tins and baking equipment.

Above the terraces in the walled garden stands Jack (*frontispiece*). *She* is a big lead statue so named by my brother Diarmid when he was small. She looks down over the garden and its profusion of flowers and vegetables. Beyond her is an archway which leads to the swimming pool and the yew hedge changing rooms (*page 81*) and the traditional home of the beehives. The gazebo (*page 69*) has a dome of green copper and is festooned with hops. As children we all had to pick the hops for the brewing of brown ale, directed by my father. This was a highly exciting event in the Biddesden kitchen. A cauldron would be placed on the big black range and it would be stirred with a special brewing paddle, which we all imagined was designed for a canoe. Elaborate readings of thermometers and saccharometers would be taken and when the fermentation was at the right stage the vat would be put into position in the corner of the front hall below General Webb and kept warm with rugs and hot water bottles and duffle coats. Meanwhile the aroma of brewing would spread through the house bringing childhood

INTRODUCTION

reminders of the Guinness brewery in Dublin where my father learnt to brew. The home brew has not been made for a few years now but my father does continue to make home-made yoghurt with similar ceremony.

As you go through the garden gate towards Jack and the gazebo there is a Mirabelle plum tree, planted to celebrate my birth. It is now very large and produces lots of pinkish gold plums every year. I was not called after a plum tree though. I was named after the tiny Shetland pony called Mirabelle because of her colour, and she was a miniature version of Plum, our vast Suffolk Punch whose job during the war was to pull the hay carts. Below the fruit trees is the huge array of vegetables and herbs. These include some fairly obscure varieties of common vegetables like Lamb's Lettuce and Pink Fir Apple Potatoes, the seeds of which are brought back by my father from his annual trips abroad.

Below the vegetable garden is the milking parlour where the Ayrshire cows produce delicious milk and cream for the house. Cream is of great importance to Biddesden cooking and my father argues that it makes you thin. I think though that this could only possibly make sense if you use cream instead of, rather than as well as, butter. Another theory is that if you have a very rich creamy pudding you need extra cream at the table to thin it down. Likewise, if the pudding is simple it will need extra cream to enhance it.

Our knowledge of food traditions does not go back very far. We can only guess that the oyster shells in the back garden are from the General's feasting. Now nearly all ingredients of Biddesden cooking are home-grown. Variety is added by pheasants and other game, by blackberries, mushrooms and hazelnuts and wild crab-apple trees, as well as walnuts which were planted by my father. Ever since my brother Finn asked for a hen for his second birthday, Biddesden has been surrounded by poultry of every shape and size. The *Poulets de Bresse* are the most delicious to eat and are very good layers too.

The recipes illustrate how the whole family involve themselves one way or another in cooking; this has resulted in a very broad range collected over many years from a wide variety of sources. Thus the Frog Sauce was introduced to my father in Damascus during the last war by Simone Thibault-Chambault, a Frenchman he met while stationed there. Other influences have been brought into the family through marriage: Indian cooking began to appear soon after my eldest sister Rosaleen married Sudhir Mulji. And of course through the years the different cooks who have run the kitchen have left many favourite and often repeated recipes. My earliest memories are of Mr and Mrs Green. I particularly remember one day there was the most tremendous commotion in the kitchen where it turned out that Mrs Green was giving in her notice having discovered a moorhen nesting in the larder. However she was to stay on until retirement and is well remembered for her *Floating Island* recipe. We often had temporary cooks and my recollection of these figures is very strong, perhaps because of the relaxation of discipline in the kitchen. I certainly remember Mrs Flanagan from Dublin encouraging me to dance on the kitchen table, and the ballet-dancer chef, D'Este, who cooked on tip-toes and had an Alsation dog whose teeth he used to clean. Elsie Tiller was responsible for introducing stylishness in presentation and

INTRODUCTION

Pink Sauce to go with fish and chips, while it remains a great treat when Rhoda cooks and we have Welsh Cakes for tea. A tribute to our cook Mr Olley is that although we have the recipe for his ginger cake nobody has been able to make it as delicious as he did. It has always been a Herculean task to cook at Biddesden because there are often at least twenty people for lunch; nowadays wonderful Val never lets us down, with the same stamina that she used to walk all the way from Appleshaw and back every day when she first worked at the house.

The cooks and the recipes all have one thing in common: they depend on cream from the dairy, vegetables from the garden and animals from the farm. As a child my father often contemplated some words written on the beer mug in which his father used to keep his shaving brush:

> Let the wealthy and great
> Roll in splendour and state
> I envy them not I declare it:
> I eat my own lamb, my own chickens and ham,
> I shear my own fleece and I wear it;
> I have lawns, I have bowers,
> I have fruits, I have flowers
> The lark is my morning alarmer.
> So jolly boys now,
> Here's God speed the plough,
> Long life and success to the farmer.

It is at Biddesden that my father made real the picture conjured up by this poem.

Soups

Vichyssoise

4 big leeks
1 onion
2 pints of chicken stock
2 medium potatoes
1 tablespoon chopped chives
1—2 oz butter
¼ pint thick cream

Chop leeks, onions and potatoes. Melt butter and add the leeks and onions and cook until soft. Add potatoes and stir. Pour in stock and simmer until potatoes are soft. Approximately 30 minutes. Process and when cool add cream, season and chill for 12 hours. Garnish with chopped chives and serve.
Serves eight.

Spinach Soup

2 lbs spinach or sorrel
1 onion
1 medium potato
2 pints of stock/ milk
1½ oz butter
seasoning
cream

Prepare and chop the onion and potato and fry until the onion is transparent in butter. Add the shredded spinach and stock and boil till potato is cooked. Process in magimix. Return to saucepan. Add milk and ¼ pint cream to taste and season. Reheat but do not boil.

This recipe can be used for lettuce or sorrel in season. Sorrel can be quite strong and so can be used as a delicious combination with spinach.
Serves four.

SOUPS

Cream of Watercress Soup

2 onions
1 potato
3 bunches of watercress
1½ oz butter

2 pints of chicken stock or
1 pint stock and 1 pint of milk
½ pint cream

Wash watercress and leave aside some leaves for decoration. Cut the tough ends off the stalks. Chop the onions and potatoes and fry in butter till onions are transparent. Add stock and cook till potatoes are soft. Add watercress towards the end so that it wilts.

Process and return to saucepan. Add cream and seasoning and reheat but do not boil. Garnish and serve.   Serves four.

Borsch

1 potato
1 onion
1 oz of butter

2 pints of stock
1 lb of cooked beetroot
2-3 tablespoons thick cream

Beetroot must be cooked by boiling till soft without breaking the skin. If it is broken the colour bleeds out. Peel and chop the cooked beetroot and the potato. Peel and finely chop the onion. Melt the butter and soften the onion for approximately 5 minutes, add potato and a little stock and boil till potato is cooked. Add beetroot and process. Reheat, season and serve adding cream at the last moment so that you get a contrast of colours.   Serves four.

Potato Soup

3 lbs potatoes
2 onions, medium
2 pints of milk or
1 pint of milk and 1 pint of water
1 ½ oz of butter
small bunch of chopped chervil or parsley
salt and pepper
grated nutmeg to taste

Chop the vegetables and fry over gentle heat until onions are transparent, keeping the lid on to retain heat and moisture —shake from time to time. Add stock and cook till potatoes are soft.

Process. Return to saucepan, season and add milk and reheat but do not boil. If it still seems too thick add more milk or water. Season, add herbs and nutmeg and serve.

To make carrot soup, substitute some of the potatoes for carrots, i.e. a ratio of half and half and use stock instead of milk. To make leek soup, use 3 lbs of leeks, 1 medium onion and 1–2 potatoes.

The ratio of vegetables does not matter. It is a question of taste. Also if a smooth consistency is not required it is better to mash the soup by hand rather than process it.

Serves six.

Cold Tomato Soup

2 lbs ripe tomatoes
¼ small onion
Juice of ½ a lemon
½ cucumber, diced
¼ pint of double cream (optional)
1 tablespoon of salt
1 tablespoon of sugar
tabasco to taste

Skin the tomatoes by pouring boiling water over them. (This will loosen the skins and make them easy to peel). Blend with ¼ small onion in magimix. Chill.

Just before serving, add salt, sugar, lemon juice and beat until smooth. Peel and dice the cucumber. Add to tomato with fresh cream and stir.

Serves four.

Starters

Taramasalata

½ pint (approximately) double or
single cream, whipped
8 oz of smoked cod's roe
lemon juice to taste
black pepper
1 tablespoon of olive oil

Open the roe and scrape away as much of the inside as you can from the skin. Put it in a mixing bowl and add the olive oil and approximately ⅓ pint of cream (preferably double) and mix until smooth and creamy. If it still tastes too strong, add more cream. Add lemon juice and black pepper to taste.

Serves four.

Rhoda's Avocado Mousse

3 avocados
2 tablespoons mayonnaise
⅓ pint of water
1 teaspoon chopped onion
lemon juice to taste

9 oz marinated prawns
 (see Finn's Prawn Cocktail)
½ packet of gelatine
seasoning to taste

Peel the avocados and process smooth. Dissolve gelatine in hot water and mix together with avocados, mayonnaise, lemon juice and onion. Oil 2 ring moulds, fill with the mixture and set aside to chill and set. Turn out and fill centre with prawns marinated with French dressing.

Serves four.

STARTERS

Cheese Soufflé

2 tablespoons of butter
2 tablespoons of flour
½ pint of milk
3 egg yolks

6 egg whites
6 oz grated cheese (Cheddar)
salt and pepper
1 teaspoon mustard powder

Melt the butter in a double boiler. Add sifted flour slowly and stir to a paste. Heat the milk and when hot add to the butter and flour and continue to cook till smooth and thick. Remove from heat. Add egg yolks alternately with cheese. Mix and heat to melt cheese.

Add salt and pepper and mustard, stir and allow to cool. Whisk egg whites until they are stiff (but not dry) and fold into warm cheese. Bake in a preheated oven 35–40 minutes at 350°F.
Serves four.

Cheese Custards

2 yolks
2 whole eggs
3 oz grated cheese (Cheddar)
1 pint of milk/cream to taste
seasoning

Mix eggs with cream/milk. Add cheese and seasoning. Pour into ramekins. Place in a large baking dish filled with hot water and steam in the medium hot oven until set. Approximately 20–30 minutes. Remove from oven (beware of hot steam when opening the door) and serve immediately. Serves six.

STARTERS

Finn's Prawn Cocktail

9 oz boiled prawns, preferably fresh
1 crispy lettuce (iceberg)
3-4 sweet eating apples
4 heaped tablespoons mayonnaise
1 little garlic
2 heaped teaspoons of tomato puree
3½ tablespoons cream
1 heaped teaspoon horseradish sauce

Prawn Marinade
1 tablespoon olive oil
1 tablespoon lemon juice
black pepper
1-2 drops tabasco

Wash and dry prawns thoroughly. Mix and marinate them for several hours. Mix the mayonnaise with the tomato puree and the horseradish and garlic, taste to check tomato/mayonnaise ratio. Stir in the cream. Remember cream will lighten the colour. Refrigerate for two or more hours.

Mix prawns with sauce, leaving a few aside for decoration. Wash and shred crispy lettuce (e.g. iceberg) and chop up eating apples into small squares. Place in cocktail glasses and add prawn mix. Decorate with extra prawns. Serve.

If you want to make the sauce stronger add more tomato or horseradish. The quality of the prawns is all important. Eschew the frozen ones if at all possible.

Serves eight.

Mirabel's Steamed Fish Starter

3 skinned and filleted lemon soles
½ pint of cream
3 eggs
juice of 1 lemon
nutmeg
seasoning
parsley
prawns for decoration

Process fish in the magimix. Add cream, eggs and chopped parsley. Season to taste. Process again and pour into greased ramekins. Decorate the top of each with prawns and place in a hot preheated oven, in a large dish of water. Cook until firm (approximately 10–15 minutes).

Serve with a quick hollandaise sauce:

3 egg yolks
juice of 1 lemon
1 tablespoon of white wine vinegar
6 oz hot skimmed melted butter
salt
cayenne pepper to taste
teaspoon of sugar

Process eggs together with seasoning and sugar. Heat the lemon juice and vinegar to boiling and pour over eggs slowly with machine on. Then add hot butter and pour out into a serving dish and serve immediately.

Serves six to eight.

STARTERS

Tomato Water Ice

2½ lbs fresh tomatoes
9 oz fresh skinned prawns
½ small onion
juice of 1 lemon
½ teaspoon sugar
seasoning

Prawn Marinade
1 tablespoon olive oil
1 tablespoon lemon juice
black pepper
1-2 drops of tabasco

Marinate the skinned prawns for 3–4 hours. Skin the tomatoes and process with peeled onion. Add lemon juice, sugar and season. If you like a sharper flavour of tomato you can add a tablespoon of tomato puree at this stage, but it will make the tomato taste less delicate.

Place in ramekins and freeze for 3–4 hours. Stir occasionally to prevent water crystals forming. Serve with a spoonful of fresh marinated prawns on the top of each dish.

There was a famous time when my parents were giving an important business dinner in New York and asked for tomato water ice to be the starter. As the hosts they were the last to be served and thus the last to taste the ice which in fact had been made as sweet and creamy as for a pudding. This recipe should have been followed.

Louise's Chicken Liver Paté

2 lbs of chicken livers
5 oz butter
2 tablespoons of port
1 tablespoon cooking brandy
fresh thyme, 3 rather large sprigs
ground mace to taste
1 teaspoon of mustard
salt and pepper to season
a small clove of garlic, chopped or crushed with salt

Melt 2 oz butter in a frying pan. Stir in livers and fry until brown outside but still pink on the inside. Process till smooth. Pour port into frying pan, add brandy, let bubble for 2 minutes, add to magimix and add rest of ingredients and extra brandy to taste. Process again and turn out into serving dish. Seal with melted butter and serve with toast. Serves eight.

Creamed Haddock

5 fillets of fresh smoked haddock
1 pint of cream

Put fillets into a bowl and pour a kettle of boiling water over them. Leave for 3-4 minutes. Drain and flake carefully, removing all the bones, any hard pieces and the skin. Place in small buttered ramekins. Pour over and cover with double cream. For a main course you can put the fish in one buttered baking dish and pour all the cream over it. Season with freshly ground black pepper and parsley and bake for approximately 12 minutes. Brown under the grill before serving. This can serve either as a tasty starter in small dishes or as a main course. Serves eight.

Sauces

Poulet à la Grenouille

garlic to taste
2 onions
1 cooked carrot
1 bunch of parsley
thyme
butter
tomatoes
tomato purée

1 cooked potato
¼-½ pint of vegetable stock
2 glasses white wine
1 wine glass of brandy
cream
salt and pepper
cayenne pepper
saffron

This sauce is suitable for prawns, ham, chicken—and also frogs. The recipe comes from Simone Thibault-Chambault, whom Bryan knew in Damascus during the war. He used the sauce for frogs caught on the Damascus to Beirut road; at Biddesden it has been used mostly with chicken.

Finely chop some garlic and two onions, parsley and a little thyme. Soften in a pan in butter. Add 3 or 4 fresh tomatoes and 2 spoonfuls of tomato purée. Add 1 cooked potato and the carrot to thicken the sauce. Moisten with vegetable stock and white wine. Process. Flambé with the brandy. At this stage strain if desired but it is not necessary. Add fresh cream and butter and saffron, also a little salt and pepper and cayenne pepper.

For frogs: brown in butter then add them to the sauce.
For prawns: boil in court bouillon and add to sauce.
For chicken and ham: Boil with vegetables, then add sauce.

Parsley Sauce

1½ oz butter
1½ oz plain flour
1 pint of stock

salt and pepper
1 heaped tablespoon finely chopped parsley

This is a traditional favourite Biddesden sauce. It can also be made with chervil which has a much more delicate flavour. It is very good served with steamed chicken and vegetables or fish or pink meat.

Melt the butter over a low heat. Add the sifted flour and reheat allowing it to sizzle for 1–2 minutes. Remove from heat and start adding ½ the boiling stock very slowly, stirring all the time to stop lumps forming. Return to heat and stir briskly while it thickens. Add the rest of the liquid, according to how thick a sauce is required. Boil sauce for 3 minutes, add parsley and whisk in the butter, a little at a time.

Cumberland Sauce

1 lemon
glass of port
1 teaspoon powdered ginger
1 orange
½ cup redcurrant jelly
½ teaspoon dry mustard
pinch of cayenne pepper

Grate the rind of the orange and lemon (carefully avoid the pith). Simmer in water for 10 minutes or until tender. Add port, jelly, mustard, ginger and pepper. Simmer until jelly has melted. Add the juice of the lemon and orange. Reheat and serve.

Bread Sauce

1 large onion
6 cloves
1 blade mace
bay leaf
large pinch ground nutmeg
2 oz brown bread crumbs
½ pint milk
1 tablespoon cream
seasoning to taste

Biddesden Bread Sauce is remarkable for two things. It is often made with brown bread, and also is produced in a sizeable quantity.

Chop the onion into small pieces. Leave one large piece and stud it with the cloves. Put it all into the milk with all the spices and bring them slowly to the boil. Remove from the heat, cover the pan and allow the pan to stand and infuse for ½ hour or so. Remove the onion with the cloves, and the bay leaf and mace. Add the bread crumbs, stir, and season.

SAUCES

Return to a low heat and allow the bread crumbs to soak up the milk. Add more milk if you think that it is becoming too thick. Keep stirring to keep a smooth consistency and also to stop the sauce from sticking to the bottom of the pan. Just before serving stir in the cream. Ideal to accompany roast turkey, chicken, pheasants.

Mirabel's Spaghetti Sauce

1 large onion
1 clove of garlic to taste
½ lb of ham or bacon
½ lb of peas
½ pint cream

olive oil
parmesan
salt
freshly ground black pepper

Heat olive oil and fry a large chopped onion and clove of garlic till soft. Crispen bacon in a frying pan. Chop bacon into small pieces and add to the onion. Add peas and stir. Peas do not need cooking very long. Add ½ pint of cream and remove from heat.

Boil the spaghetti very free in plenty of well salted water and a dash of olive oil on top for approximately 3-5 minutes. Strain and add to the sauce in a heated bowl. If it seems too dry add more cream. Add parmesan cheese and plenty of freshly ground black pepper.

The spaghetti must not be overcooked. Test frequently to avoid this. Remember that it does go on cooking after being strained. It should be *al dente*, just tender but firm to the bite. Allow 3-4 oz per person for main course and less if it is for a starter. Serves four.

Horseradish Sauce

¼ pint of cream
squeeze of lemon
1-1½ heaped tablespoons of freshly grated horseradish
salt and pepper
1 tablespoon of wine vinegar
½ teaspoon of mustard powder
sugar to taste

Soak the grated horseradish in the vinegar for 10–15 minutes. Mix in the lemon, mustard, seasoning and sugar. Whip cream until stiff and add. Adjust the seasoning (if you can take the taste) and possibly add more horseradish if it is needed. It goes a long way.

SAUCES

Fiona's Rowan Berry Jelly

Rowan berries
Cane sugar (granulated)

Pick rowan berries, clean and wash in cold water. Put them in a saucepan and just cover with cold water. Bring to boil and simmer slowly for an hour or so, mashing with a potato masher as soon as soft enough. When the fruit is thoroughly puréed, strain it through a double layer of muslin. At this stage you can squeeze as much juice out as possible as it won't matter if the juice is cloudy.

Return the dry (squeezed) fruit to the saucepan, add some more water, and mash again. This double processing ensures that as much juice as possible is obtained from the fruit since rowan berries do not give up their juice easily. Strain the fruit again and when it is thoroughly squeezed wash the muslin and discard the fruit.

Now strain the juice, without squeezing, through four layers of muslin and a beautifully clear pink juice will be produced. Measure the quantity of juice and put it in a very large saucepan, leaving plenty of room for expansion and the addition of sugar, and bring to the boil. Remove from heat and add warmed sugar at the ratio of 1 lb of sugar per 1 pint of juice. Stir until the sugar is thoroughly dissolved. Return to heat and boil as fast as possible, skimming now and then with a wooden spoon.

Heat up some clean, dry jam jars with good sealing screw lids in the oven. When the juice is ready it will set on a cold plate. Skim for the last time and withdraw from heat. Pour juice immediately into the hot jars and seal with lids straight away. This will ensure that the jelly is sterile and a vacuum will be formed when cool. Put jelly away in a cool place where it won't get jogged while setting.

This recipe is also good if you substitute some cooking apples for the rowans. It helps the jelly set and softens the taste of rowan. I recommend a ratio of up to ½ and ½. (MJH)

Pink Sauce

cream
tomato ketchup
salt and pepper

Served with fish, usually fried. Beat the cream until stiff. Mix in tomato ketchup until the sauce is pale pink in colour. Add salt and pepper to taste.

Vegetables

Catriona's Carrots

2 lbs of carrots
2 teaspoons brown sugar
1 oz butter
parsley
bay leaf
½ pint water
salt
juice of 1 lemon

Prepare carrots shaped as you wish; if new and small they can stay whole. Put in a pan with the bay leaf and water, 2 pinches of salt and the sugar. Cover and boil until tender which, depending on the age of the carrots, is from 15-20 minutes. Remove lid to let all steam and excess water evaporate and remove from heat. Add butter and when carrots start to sizzle in the butter add a squeeze of lemon juice. Sprinkle with chopped parsley. Serves six.

Potato and Basil

2 lbs of new potatoes
4 tablespoons olive oil
1 handful of fresh basil leaves
juice of ½-1 lemon

Marinate the basil with the lemon juice and olive oil and seasoning for 1 hour or more. Scrub (and skin if desired) the potatoes, cut them if necessary to make them roughly the same size. Plain boil until cooked. Drain and toss in marinade and serve immediately.

Serves six.

SAUCES

Roast Potatoes

If you like them soft with the flavour of the meat, cook them with the roast, but actually they will always crispen better if they can be cooked separately at the top of the oven.

Prepare the potatoes and part boil for 5 minutes. Strain and leave aside for another 5 minutes for the steam to dry off them. Place in hot oil at the top of the oven for approximately 1 hour according to the size of potato. Turn them after half time. You can add herbs, i.e. rosemary or garlic, to the hot oil for flavour if needed.

Onions *à la Grècque*

1 lb of onions (ideally all of same size)
¼ pint water
¼ pint white wine
juice of half a lemon
4 tablespoons of olive oil
1 tablespoon of chopped parsley
2 tablespoons of tomato purée
2 tablespoons of sugar
1 sprig of rosemary
salt and pepper to taste

Put all the ingredients except the parsley in a saucepan with the peeled but whole onions and bring to the boil. Simmer for about ½ an hour or until the onions are cooked. Lift them out taking care to keep them whole and place in the serving dish. Boil the cooking liquid rapidly to reduce for 5–10 minutes, until nearly half the original quantity. Pour over the onions and leave to cool. Sprinkle the chopped parsley over before serving cold.   Serves four to six.

Rhoda's Baked Cabbage

1 large cabbage
1 pint of cream
salt and pepper

Cut cabbage into quarters, partially boil for 5 minutes. Place in a buttered baking dish, season with salt and freshly ground pepper, pour over the cream and cover with foil. Bake in a medium oven for approximately 1 hour.

Serves six to eight.

Tamsy's Apple Salad

10 sweet eating apples   *mayonnaise*
4 medium sized carrots   *lemon juice*
3 oz of walnuts (2 handfuls)

Chop apples into ½ inch squares, grate carrots and add the walnuts. Stir in enough mayonnaise to cover all the apple. Add a squeeze of lemon juice.

Serves six.

Catriona's Brussels Sprouts

1½-2 lbs prepared Brussels sprouts
1 tablespoon of honey
seasoning

Prepare the Brussels sprouts by trimming the base and removing the outer loose leaves and any yellow leaves. Make a cross at the base with knife to even up the cooking. Rinse with cold water.

Steam for 5-10 minutes with the lid on. Time depends on the size of the sprouts; but they should still be crunchy. Place in a heated bowl and spoon the honey over them, season and serve hot. Serves four.

Rosaleen's Kidney Beans with Ginger

2 cups kidney beans
10 cups water
3 onions
1 clove garlic
about 2 cubic inches of fresh root ginger oil (e.g. Saffola)
2 teaspoons jeera powder (cumin)
1 teaspoon dhania powder (coriander)

Pick through the beans to remove any suspect ones or bits of stones or dirt. Rinse and then add 5 times their volume of cold water and soak overnight, preferably in a pan which can be used both on top of the stove and in an oven.

SAUCES

Bring to the boil slowly and boil hard for 10 minutes. Add boiling water if necessary. Cover and cook in an oven which is hot enough to keep the beans simmering. Cook for at least 1 ½ hours. (The older and drier the beans the longer the cooking time).

Peel and finely chop the ginger and garlic. Heat oil and fry them with the jeera and dhania powder. Add sliced onions and cook till soft. Add this to the beans when these are really soft through and through. Mix thoroughly. Add salt and freshly ground black pepper to taste and cook for 5 minutes or so.

Any left-over beans should be eaten cold next day mixed with yogurt. Serves six.

Main Courses

Calf's Liver with Herbs and Mushrooms

liver
mushrooms
onions
garlic to taste

flour and seasonings
butter
thyme
lemon

This is a very simple, traditional way of serving liver. The mushroom and herb mixture is the old fashioned version of *fines herbes*.

To every sliver of liver, allow half a dozen medium sized mushrooms and a medium to large sized onion. Chop the mushrooms, onions and garlic. Fry the onions in butter until transparent in a frying pan. Season the liver, dust with flour and add to the frying pan with a little extra butter. Let the liver take colour quickly on both sides, then add the mushrooms and thyme to taste and continue to cook for 3 minutes over a very gentle heat, taking care it does not stick. Do not overcook. Serve with a squeeze of lemon.

Venison Marinade

To 2 lb of meat: *1 large onion*
1 desert spoon juniper berries
½ teaspoon ground bay leaf
1 teaspoon black peppercorns

1 clove garlic (optional)
½ pint red wine or Guinness
2 tablespoons olive oil
Seasoning

Venison tends to dry out and be quite tough unless it is cooked with care and marinated preferably as long as overnight.

MAIN COURSES

Pot roasting is an ideal way of cooking venison to prevent the meat drying out too much and keep the flour and juices in, with vegetables as well as the marinade. For ordinary roasting allow 25 minutes per lb and roast in a moderate oven to 350° F.

To marinate the meat, place the venison in a deep dish. Slice the onion and crush the juniper berries and sprinkle them over the meat with the ground bay leaf and pepper corns. Pour either the red wine or Guinness over the top with the olive oil so that the meat is well covered. It is a good idea to turn the meat over after about 4 hours.

Rosaleen's Ham

1 ham
1 inch root ginger
1 desert spoon of mustard powder
2 tablespoons brown sugar
2 lb carrots
1-2 large onions
cloves
juice of 2 oranges
1 bottle of Guinness

Soak a scrubbed smoked ham overnight in cold water. Place in fresh water with prepared carrots and onions and peppercorns. Bring to the boil. Simmer, allowing 20 minutes to the lb. (Do not stick anything into the ham at this stage.) Allow to cool in the water. When cool, lift it out of the water and peel off the skin.

Press the freshly grated ginger, mustard and brown sugar into the surface and stud it with cloves. Bake in a hot oven for about 20 minutes, basting it with Guinness and orange juice. Dredge it with more brown sugar and cook again on lower heat for another half an hour without basting.

Chicken Italian

2 chickens, skinned and jointed
8 medium sized onions
1-2 cloves of garlic (to taste)
8 lbs tomatoes, skinned, fresh in preference to tinned
1 cup of olive oil
1 cup of white wine vinegar/ lemon juice
fresh herbs, eg basil
chicken stock

Fry the jointed chicken until crispy on the outside in olive oil. Add onions, stirring the chickens to the top from time to time and adding oil to stop it sticking. When the onions are soft, add the tomatoes, seasoning and ½ pint or so of chicken stock. Return to heat. Soften the tomatoes. Do not overcook or allow the tomatoes to reduce and taste too strong. Liquidize tomato sauce if preferred and pour over chicken before serving.

Before removing from heat, add 1 cup olive oil and 1 cup of vinegar to tomato sauce and fresh herbs to taste. Serve with mashed potatoes.

Chicken Elizabeth

1 roasted chicken
¼ pint cream
½ pint mayonnaise

Curry Paste
1 tablespoon apricot jam
1 tablespoon honey
1 desert spoon of curry powder
1 teaspoon of tomato purée
1 cooking apple
1 onion
1 glass dry white wine
Salt and pepper
Small glass of water

Skin and chop the onion and apple and gently cook till the onion is soft. Add jam, curry powder, tomato purée, wine, water and honey. Cook for 15 minutes. Process and cool. Whip cream and add ½ pint of mayonnaise. Mix with the curry paste.

Prepare the cooked chicken and cut into pieces of desired size, carefully removing skin and bone. Place in a dish and cover with the sauce. Sprinkle with browned nuts and serve with rice.

Roast Pork with Cider and Apple Jelly

leg or loin of pork
seasoning
1 lb pot of apple jelly

1 pint of cider
Thyme

This recipe might mean forfeiting the crackling, so it is suggested that the skin is cut as for crackling and sliced off and

MAIN COURSES

placed at the top of the oven to crispen up in another dish.

Rub the meat with salt, pepper and thyme. Place in a hot oven (450° F) for the first 10 minutes. Reduce the heat to 395° F and add the cider and apple jelly and continue to baste until the meat is cooked. Approximately 1 ½ hours at 350°F or 25 minutes to the lb.

Add water or cider to roasting dish to make gravy, season and thicken to taste.

Mirabel's Pigeon Casserole

pigeons
onions, medium sized
carrots, medium sized
blackcurrant jam
red wine
seasoning
stock/water

One pigeon per person depending on appetite.

Put a tablespoon of blackcurrant jam inside each pigeon. Chop up the carrots and onions. Soften the onions in a little butter in the casserole, add the pigeons and carrots and toss them over the heat for 2 minutes. Add a tumbler of red wine and a tumbler of water, season and place in a medium oven (300°F) for 2 hours. Season and serve when the meat is tender. Do not overcook because if the bird falls apart the bones are very small and annoying.

Chicken Maryland

4 chicken joints
2 oz self raising flour
1 beaten egg and breadcrumbs
2 oz butter or bacon fat
½ pint of stock
½ teaspoon salt
¼ teaspoon of pepper

Toss the chicken in seasoned flour, then coat with egg and breadcrumbs. Leave aside for 1 hour to allow the coat to settle. Melt the fat in a heavy pan. Brown the chicken joints, reduce heat and cook very gently until the chicken is tender. About ½ an hour. Add more butter if it starts to stick in the pan. Serve with corn fritters and fried bananas.

MAIN COURSES

The fritters are made in the following way: make a batter with 2 oz of self-raising flour, salt, 1 egg and 4 tablespoons of milk. Stir in sweet corn from a 5 oz tin and fry tablespoons of the mixture in hot oil until crisp and golden brown.

Georgian Pheasant

1 pheasant
3 oz walnuts
2 lbs grapes (white)
4 oranges, preferably bloody
¾ pint sweet Muscadet wine
tea bag - green tea
¼ pint of cream

Shell the walnuts. The skin can be loosened by pouring boiling water over them, to remove bitterness. De-pip the grapes and process and sieve. Squeeze the oranges.

Make tea with ¼ pint of water, leave to brew for 5 minutes. Put pheasant in casserole with grapes, walnuts, orange juice and tea so that pheasant is almost covered. Season and cover.

Bake for 50 minutes at 350°-375 °F. Remove the pheasant and walnuts onto a serving dish. Reduce juices to ½, add cream and pour over the carved pheasant or serve as a gravy.

Roast Duck

2 ducks
½ pint of red wine
Juice of one orange or lemon
1 onion, large
1 tablespoon of brandy
1 orange cut in quarters
Salt
Pepper

Prepare the ducks by pricking the skin well all over and rubbing with salt.

Squeeze out the juice of the orange or lemon. In each duck place ½ an orange quartered and ½ a peeled onion. Roast in a very hot oven for the first 20 minutes on a rack so that the fat can drip separately. Wild ducks aren't as fat as duckling from the butcher so may not need this treatment. Pour fat out of baking dish and add wine and orange juice and salt and pepper. Place the ducks in the dish to roast at 350°F for another 10 – 15 minutes or until cooked. Remove the juices to reduce and season for gravy. Add brandy to taste.

Normandy Pheasant

To every pheasant:	*juice of half a lemon*
4 large cooking apples	*2 oz butter*
¼ bottle of white wine	*salt and black pepper*
¼ pint of cream	*Calvados (optional)*

Put the butter in a casserole and sauté the pheasant whole until nicely browned all over. Meanwhile add the peeled and sliced apples. When both are brown, add wine, cover and cook in a moderate oven 375°F for half an hour. Add cream and lemon juice and season to taste with black pepper and salt. Continue to cook until the bird is tender, maybe another 15 minutes. For extra flavour stuff the pheasant with another peeled apple. Calvados can be added to the cream before serving. This recipe is very good for pigeons and other game, as well as chickens and guinea fowl.

Serves four to six per pheasant.

Louise and Sachin's Prawns

2 medium size onions
1 lb of fresh prawns
½ block coconut cream
¾ pint boiling water
1 teaspoon cumin
4 ground cardamom pods
2 teaspoons of coriander
2 teaspoons of turmeric

2 teaspoons of chilli powder
1 teaspoon of poppy seeds, optional
lime juice to taste
1 inch root ginger
3 tablespoons of sunflower oil
lemon juice
salt and pepper

Chop onions, peel and slice the ginger and fry in olive oil for 2–3 minutes. Add the cumin, cardamom, coriander, turmeric, chilli powder and poppy seeds and stir. Add the prawns. Make the coconut milk by mixing the block of coconut cream with boiling water. Add and heat moderately for 5–10 minutes. Do not overcook the prawns. Add a squeeze of lemon juice at the end. Season with salt and freshly ground black pepper. Serve with Basmati Rice.

Puddings

Ginger Cream

A packet of thin ginger wafers or ginger thin biscuits
1 pint of double cream

Whisk cream until firm. Pack the biscuits along the dish with cream spread in between. Cover the long sausage of biscuits with the rest of the cream and leave overnight in the fridge. Serve with lashings of runny cream.
Serves six to eight.

Baked Alaska

2 pints of ice cream
 any flavour, vanilla is best
1 round plain sponge cake - 6-8" diameter
3 whites of egg
6 oz or less of caster sugar
1 good wine glass of sweet white wine or a little less Kirsch,
    Grand Marnier or fresh orange juice.

Place the sponge cake in a serving dish (a quiche dish shape is best) and soak in the wine. Preheat the oven to very hot. Whisk the eggs and sugar to a meringue consistency. Pile the ice cream evenly on top of the sponge. Cover completely with the meringue. Dust with castor sugar and place in a pre-heated hot oven for 2-3 minutes or until the meringue is nicely coloured. Serve immediately before the ice cream melts.

Louise's Gooseberry Fool

1 lb gooseberries (young)
4 elderflowers
1 oz butter

¼ pint double cream
2 oz sugar

Top and tail the gooseberries. Put in a dish with the elderflowers, the sugar and the butter and cook for ¾ hour in a medium oven, 300° F, or until the fruit is soft. Remove the elderflower stalks, mash or process the gooseberries and cool. Add ¼ pint of whipped double cream. Serve chilled.

Serves six to eight.

Lemon Delight

2 oz butter
4 tablespoonfuls of sugar
2 oz flour
rind and juice of 2 lemons

cup of milk
2 egg yolks
3 egg whites beaten stiff

Blend the butter and the sugar. Add the beaten yolk of eggs and the grated rind of lemons. Add the lemon juice, the flour and the cup of milk. Mix them all well together. Add the whites of eggs, beaten very stiff as for meringues and mix them in. Put into a buttered dish and bake in a moderate oven till golden brown.

Orange Delight may be made similarly using the rind (with more of the zest) and juice of oranges.

The recipe improves if cooked in a dish standing in about 1" of water. This forms a more liquid consistency at the bottom of the pudding giving it a more interesting and contrasting effect.

Hedgehog

This recipe originates from a ballet dancer chef we once had called D'Esté. Make about a dozen crêpe type pancakes. Place on top of each other with a layer of apple puree between each pancake. Top with a layer of nuts. Walnuts are good for this though the original recipe used almonds stuck in upright to give a prickly effect—hence its name.

Catriona's Crumble

4 oz plain flour
3 oz butter
3 oz brown sugar
pinch of cinnamon
3 digestive biscuits

Rub the butter and flour together and stir in the sugar and crushed biscuits. Sprinkle on top of fruit in baking dish and bake at 375°F or mark 5 for 10 minutes, then lower to 350°F or mark 4 for 35 minutes.

The fruit consists of chunky pieces of chopped apple, mixed with a tablespoon of soft brown sugar, lemon rind, cinnamon, cloves and spices and lemon juice particularly around the edge of the dish.

Toffee Pudding

½ lb butter
1 small tin of golden syrup
½ pint of milk
6-8 thick slices of yesterday's white bread

Put milk at the bottom of a large flat dish and soak the pieces of bread, turning the bread until it is saturated. Put butter and syrup into a frying pan over a low heat and stir until melted together. Boil rapidly until it starts to change colour. Remove bread and place in hot toffee till well coated and crisp on each side. Remove into a heated serving dish and pour excess syrup over to taste. Serve with cream.

Soufflé Glacé au Grand Marnier

2½ fl. oz of Grand Marnier
juice of 1 lemon and 1 orange
4 oz caster sugar
5 egg yolks
3 egg whites
¾ pint cream

Put the sugar with 2 or 3 tablespoons of water in a pan. Heat to a syrup and boil for a few minutes until it threads. "Threading" occurs when the sugar and water syrup makes a thin brittle line between finger and thumb. Pour onto the yolks and beat until thick and fluffy and cold. Stir in the Grand Marnier and the juice of the lemon and orange. Whip the cream and fold in. Whisk the egg whites until stiff, fold in and freeze.

This recipe can be used with other liqueurs. Cointreau is good though a little sweet. Grand Marnier is a Biddesden favourite. Serves six to eight.

Kieran's Chocolate Mousse

2 bars (7 oz) of Chocolat Menier
milk
6 tablespoons of caster sugar
3 eggs
3 egg whites

Melt the chocolate in a little milk. Mix the sugar with the 3 egg yolks. Beat up the 6 egg whites till very stiff. Mix chocolate, egg yolks and sugar together, then fold in egg whites.

Sachin's Hot Chocolate Soufflé

4 tablespoons plain flour
1 teaspoon cornflour
3 teaspoons caster sugar
12 egg whites, two egg yolks, two whole eggs
8 tablespoons milk

10 tablespoons double cream
⅓ lb Chocolat Menier
2 tablespoons cocoa powder
⅓ lb caster sugar (to mix when whipping egg whites)

First make the *crème patisserie*:

In a mixing bowl combine the flours and the caster sugar. In another bowl beat together the egg yolks and the whole eggs, then beat in the flour mixture, adding it gradually and mixing to a smooth paste. In a pan mix the milk with 2 tablespoons of the double cream, bring to the boil then remove from heat, add 2 oz of the Chocolat Menier, the cocoa, and mix until smooth. Gradually stir this chocolate milk into the flour paste, return to the pan and cook over a low heat beating to a smooth thick paste. Leave until cool.

Now make a *ganache*:

In a pan slowly warm the remaining 8 tablespoons of cream and beat the remaining chocolate. Remove from heat, stir until smooth and leave to cool.

Whisk the egg whites with the caster sugar. Combine the crème patisserie and the ganache and carefully fold in the egg whites with a large metal spoon in the normal way for soufflés.

Put into greased soufflé dishes, level off, garnish with orange zest and bake for 20 minutes in a moderate oven (350° F). Serve immediately with single cream.

Serves eight.

PUDDINGS

Brown Bread Ice Cream

4 oz brown bread
4 oz sugar
½ pint of double cream

2 eggs
Vanilla pod

Process the bread to breadcrumbs. Mix with half the sugar and brown in the oven stirring it from time to time.

Separate the eggs. Process the egg yolks and the remaining sugar and cream in magimix. Place in a saucepan with the vanilla pod over a low heat to allow the mixture to thicken and get the flavour of vanilla. Cool and remove the vanilla pod. Stir in breadcrumbs. Stiffly whisk the egg whites and add to mixture and freeze.

Zabaglione

5 egg yolks
1 tablespoon of sugar

4 spoonfuls of sherry or marsala or white wine

Put 5 egg yolks and sugar in a small saucepan. Whip together for 2 minutes. When nicely whipped add 4 spoonfuls of sherry or marsala or white wine (whichever preferred). Whip thoroughly.

In a larger saucepan have some boiling water. Place the small saucepan containing the mixture into the larger while the water is kept boiling continue to beat until it becomes fairly thick. Remove the smaller saucepan and whip again. Then serve in cups.

Shah of Persia

4 eggs
8 oz caster sugar
vanilla

Separate the eggs, beat the whites till very stiff, and add 3 oz sieved caster sugar. Meanwhile make a caramel by very slowly heating 3 oz sugar in a saucepan. Line a pudding basin with runny caramel, and add the egg whites. Put another bowl on top as a lid as it rises and steam gently over a saucepan of boiling water for an hour. Run a palette knife round the edge and turn out onto a dish. The caramel should slip down the sides of the egg white.

The sauce is made by beating the egg yolks with a little vanilla over a bowl of hot water. Make some more runny caramel and slowly add to the egg yolks drop by drop until it becomes a pale colour. This may be the sauce but serve it with cream too.

A variation to this recipe is to substitute a proportion of the castor sugar for equal quantities of crushed macaroons.

Mrs Green's Floating Island

2 eggs
⅔ of a pint of milk
1 teaspoon sugar

1 vanilla pod
2 oz castor sugar

This pudding consists of a rich custard with icebergs of egg white floating in it.

Custard: Heat the milk with the vanilla pod being careful not to bring it to the boil. Separate the eggs putting the whites aside in a dry mixing bowl. Lightly beat the yolks with the teaspoon of sugar. Pour milk into this egg mixture and return to heat with the vanilla pod. To avoid lumpy custard it is essential to have separated out all the egg white; otherwise it may be necessary to strain out the custard mixture before cooking. Cook very gently, stirring now and then, until a thin layer of custard coats the back of a wooden spoon. Remove the vanilla pod and pour into a dish to cool. Cover with a damp cloth to prevent a skin forming.

When the custard is cool, whisk the egg whites till stiff, then gradually add castor sugar, a little at first and continuing to beat until very firm. Put large peaked blobs of this mixture to float on the surface of the custard.   Serves 3–4 people.

Bramble Summer Pudding

1½ - 2 lbs blackberries
2-4 oz caster sugar

white bread
cream

Cook the blackberries without adding water, until pulpy. Sweeten with sugar to taste, sieve if pips undesired. Line a pudding basin with pieces of white bread without their crusts. Fill the centre with sieved blackberries (sweetened to taste) alternating the layers of bread until full. Make sure everything is well saturated with juice, with no bread showing white. Place a weighted saucer (1 lb) on top, leave to soak overnight. Turn out and cover with whipped cream. Serve with a jug of any extra juice.

The blackberries need not be sieved but many people do not like the pips so at Biddesden either we have a pipless summer pudding or 2 puddings so that we can have a choice. This recipe can be used for other soft fruit in season e.g. rhubarb, damsons, raspberries or strawberries.

Chocolate Roll

5 egg yolks
1 cup of icing sugar
3 tablespoons of cocoa

5 egg whites
whipped cream
icing sugar

Beat the egg yolks until thick. Add the sifted icing sugar and heat thoroughly. Add the cocoa and then fold in the stiffly whisked egg whites. Spread on a buttered and flavoured biscuit tray 8"x 12" and only ½" high and bake at 350°F for 10 minutes.

Turn out on grease proof paper sprinkled with caster sugar and cocoa. Cover with a wet cloth and leave in the larder or fridge, preferably overnight. Spread with whipped cream and raspberries if you like, and roll up.

PUDDINGS

Gianmarina's Pudding

1 lb of fruit – either de-pipped grapes, spooned melons, sliced fresh peaches, raspberries or strawberries

1 pint of cream, possibly more or 2 cartons of Greek yoghurt
3 heaped tablespoons of dark brown sugar

Cover the bottom of a heat proof dish thickly with fruit. Whip the cream stiff and spoon over the top of the fruit and spread level. Freeze for a short while till the cream is quite firm. Sprinkle the sugar evenly over the top and put under a preheated grill just long enough for the sugar to melt but not the cream. Serve immediately. Serves eight.

Nutty Meringue

4 oz of short crust pastry i.e.:
 4 oz plain flour
pinch of salt
2½ oz butter and/or lard
squeeze of lemon
a little water to mix

Filling:
3 egg whites
4 oz soft brown sugar
2 oz chopped walnuts

Roll the pastry out to fit a shallow 9" pie dish or plate. Pinch the bottom of the flan, cover with greaseproof paper and fill with beans or rice etc. This prevents the pastry case from losing its shape. Bake "blind" in a hot oven 400°F for about 25 minutes.

Filling. Whisk the egg whites until stiff and then fold in the sifted sugar and the nuts. Put into pastry case and bake in a cool oven (300°F) for about 1½ hours.

Guinness Christmas Pudding

10 oz fresh breadcrumbs
8 oz soft brown sugar
8 oz currants
10 oz seeded raisins (chopped)
8 oz sultanas
2 oz mixed peel (chopped)
10 oz shredded suet

½ level teaspoon salt
1 level teaspoon mixed spice
grated rind of 1 lemon
1 dessert spoon lemon juice
2 large eggs (beaten)
¼ pint of milk
1 bottle of Guinness (10 fl. ozs)

Mix all the dry ingredients together in a large basin. Stir in lemon juice, eggs, milk and Guinness. Mix well and turn into one 2 pt and one 3 pt well-greased pudding basins. Tie pudding cloths over puddings or cover them tightly with greaseproof paper and foil. Leave overnight. Steam for about 7½ hours. If not eating the puddings immediately, cool, recover and store in a cool place. When required, steam for a further 2-3 hours before serving. Serves ten to twelve people.

Blackcurrant Leaf Ice

1 pint of water
9 oz sugar
pared rind of 2 lemons
juice of 3 lemons

3-4 handfuls of blackcurrant leaves
1 egg white, whisked
a few drops of green colouring

Put the rind into a scrupulously clean saucepan with the sugar and water. Dissolve completely, then boil rapidly for 5-6 minutes. Add the washed leaves, cover and set aside to allow to infuse until a well flavoured tea has been extracted. Strain, squeezing leaves to extract all syrup. Add the juice of the lemons, stir and freeze. Remove from freezer and stir from time to time to make it as smooth as possible and when it is nearly solid add the whisked white of egg. Refreeze. The green colouring, added with the lemon juice comes from an old Biddesden recipe but it is much more traditional not to add it and to have it white. It also makes it more difficult when it is white for people to guess what ice it is. The leaves should be picked in April-May when they are young. Thus this ice is very seasonal unless you store it in a deep freeze.

Felicity's Port Jelly

4 oz sugar
1 tablespoon redcurrant jelly
1 bottle port
1 pint of water (depending on how intoxicated you want people)
juice of ½ lemon
1¾ packet of gelatine (possibly less to taste)
1 stick of cinnamon
4 cloves
pinch of ground nutmeg

This is an excellent party pudding as it is deceptively alcoholic. Dissolve the gelatine in half of the port by leaving it to soak. Dissolve the sugar and redcurrant jelly with cinnamon, cloves, nutmeg and water and a little more of the port and bring it almost to the boil. Strain and add the gelatine mixture and the rest of the port. Pour into a mould and allow to set. Excellent served chilled with lots of cream to disguise the alcoholic content. Beware.

Cakes

Rhoda's Welsh Cakes (Picau-Bach)

½ lb margarine (butter is too heavy)
6 oz sugar
1 lb self-raising flour
6 oz sultanas
2 eggs
milk – enough to mix to slightly wetter than pastry consistency

Rub margarine into flour and sugar. Add the sultanas. Break in the eggs and stir with a wooden spoon. Add milk and mix to a sticky consistency. Roll out on a floured board to ¼" thick and cut into small rounds (or other shapes). Cook on top of griddle or a heavy bottomed frying pan. They are very easily burnt by mistake. Sieve castor sugar over the top before serving for tea. Eat by themselves.

Val's Brownies

½ lb Chocolat Menier
½ lb unsalted butter
⅔ lb caster sugar
3 eggs plus 1 extra yolk, lightly beaten
2 oz plain flour
½ teaspoon baking powder
pinch of salt
2 oz cocoa powder
¼lb walnuts (optional)

Melt the chocolate in a double boiler. Beat the butter and sugar together and gradually add the eggs. Sift the flour, baking powder, salt and cocoa powder into a large bowl and mix well. Gently fold in the chocolate, followed by the dry ingredients and walnuts. Spoon the mixture into a tin and bake for 30 minutes in a moderate oven.

Melting Moments

12 oz butter
4 oz icing sugar
1 lb self-raising flour

Cream the butter and the sugar together. Add sifted flour with a pinch of salt and knead. Roll out very thin (¼″) and place on a greased baking sheet and bake at 375°F for 10-15 minutes.

Catriona's Chocolate Cake

3 oz Chocolat Menier
4 oz unsalted butter
6½ oz sugar
5 eggs
3 oz ground almonds
1½ oz self-raising flour

Icing:
5 oz chocolate
5 oz butter

Melt the chocolate and when soft, cream with the butter, sugar and egg yolks. Beat egg whites until very stiff. Fold almonds and sifted flour into the chocolate mixture and then carefully add the egg whites. Put in a greased and lined tin and bake at 375°F or Mark 4, for 45 minutes. When cooled cut in half and fill with raspberry jam (and cream if it doesn't need to keep for a long time).

Icing: Melt the chocolate and butter over a low heat, stir well, and when cool (when it is fairly firm), spread over the cake.

Elisabeth's Favourite Girdle Scones

8 oz self-raising flour
1-2 oz of fat
¼ pint of milk to mix
large pinch of salt

Sift flour and a large pinch of salt and rub in the fat. Make a well in the centre of the flour and slowly stir in enough milk with a wooden spoon to make a soft dough. Roll out onto a floured board approximately ½ inch thick and cut into shapes. Cook over a moderate heat on a greased girdle or heavy based frying pan until they are brown each side, for about 5 minutes altogether. You can add raisins to this recipe if you like.

Pain d' Epices

4½ oz caster sugar
4½ oz honey
10½ oz flour
pinch of salt
½ teaspoon of bicarbonate of soda
½ teacup of boiling water

Dissolve the honey and sugar in boiling water. Add the sifted flour, pinch of salt and bicarbonate of soda and mix well. Cook in a medium oven in a bread tin not filled more than half full for approximately 1 hour.

Mr Olley's Ginger Cake

10 oz black and golden syrups
4 oz butter
6 oz demerara sugar
2-3 level teaspoons of ground ginger
1 teaspoon of cinnamon

12 oz self raising flour
1 egg
1 teaspoon bicarbonate of soda
milk to mix
crystallized ginger and sultanas

Warm the syrups in a saucepan with the butter, sugar, ground ginger and cinnamon. Mix together the flour, egg, bicarbonate of soda and the warmed treacle mixture with a little milk to form a stiff batter in a bowl. Place crystallized ginger and sultanas in bottom of a low flat baking tin and pour the batter over this. Bake at 250°F for approximately ½ to ¾ of an hour or until there is a spongy film on top when pressed. Turn out onto an oiled piece of greaseproof paper.

Rhoda's Shortbread Biscuits

12 oz plain flour
8 oz butter (soft)
6 oz caster sugar

Knead all the ingredients together thoroughly until no longer crumbly, using castor sugar on the kneading surface. Form into a long sausage shape and cut thin slices off the end. Cook in a slow oven on a baking tray for 2-3 hours, or hotter for shorter.

CAKES

Guinness Cake

1 lb flour
½ lb butter
½ lb sugar
1½ lb fruit: raisins, cherries if desired, sultanas
1½ teaspoons of bicarbonate of soda
½ pint of Guinness

Rub the butter into the flour. Add the sugar and fruit. Dissolve the bicarbonate of soda in the Guinness and add to the mixture. Mix well and bake in a moderate oven for up to 2 hours.

Rhoda's Soda Bread

3 cups of white flour
2 cups of wholemeal flour
1 desert spoon of sugar
1 desert spoon of salt
1 teaspoon bicarbonate of soda
1 teaspoon bex tartar (cream of tartar)
Approximately 1 pint of milk

Mix dry ingredients lightly with fingers. Make a well in the middle and add some of the milk. Knead with wholemeal flour until correct consistency. Cut in half and mark with a knife. Bake at 350°F for ½ an hour, turning at 15 minutes.

Puss's Scotch Pancakes

8 oz flour
1-2 tablespoons golden syrup
pinch of salt
1 egg

½ pint of milk approximately
1½ teaspoons cream of tartar
1 teaspoon bicarbonate of soda

Mix sieved flour, salt and warmed syrup. Add the beaten egg and gradually add milk, beating into a smooth batter until it is of a dropping consistency. Beat in the sieved bicarbonate of soda and cream of tartar. Heat a heavy pan until hot and rub over with oil on a piece of paper. Drop a spoonful into the pan. This should produce a small sizzling noise. When bubbles have appeared all over the upper surface, turn. The cooked side should be of a smooth golden brown colour. On the second side it should rise evenly all over. If rising more in the centre then batter is too thick and should be thinned with more milk. The second side should also be cooked to a smooth golden brown. If it reaches this colour before the centre is cooked, then the pan is too hot.

Tamsy's Orange Cake

1 lb castor sugar
1 lb butter
8 eggs
1 lb self-raising flour

Sauce:
4-6 oranges
1 lemon
8 oz castor sugar

Cream the 1 lb of castor sugar with the butter. Mix in the eggs and the flour. Bake at 400°F for 1¼ hours (approximately). Ready when a knife comes out clean. (N.B. this cake is very easy to burn.) Turn out cake upside down on a plate.

Dissolve the 8 oz caster sugar in the juice of the oranges and lemon and add zest from the oranges. Pour this mixture over the cake.

Fiona's 'Malt' Loaf

8 oz plain flour
8 oz whole wheat flour
6 oz sugar
6 oz treacle
½ pint warm water

sultanas
nuts
pinch of salt
2 teaspoons baking powder

Warm the treacle in most of the water and allow the sultanas to soak in this. Mix the flours with the sugar, nuts and salt. Add the treacle mixture to the flour mixture and stir well. Add more water if necessary to form a nice damp consistency. Sieve in the baking powder and mix again well. Pour into a loaf tin which should be well greased and lined with butter papers. Bake in the centre of a medium oven for about ¾ hour. In order to keep the loaf moist" I usually bake it with a lid, formed by placing another tin upside down over the loaf. Should be eaten spread with butter.

Rhum Truffles

4 oz plain chocolate
½ oz butter
1 egg yolk
4 oz icing sugar
2 oz cocoa (approximately)
1-2 tablespoons of brandy

Melt the chocolate with the butter in a mixing bowl over steam. Mix in the icing sugar until smooth. Remove from heat and add the egg yolk and the brandy. Gradually blend in the cocoa until it is of a fairly stiff consistency. The exact quantity of cocoa needed will depend on the size of the egg and the quantity of brandy used.

Roll into balls. Sieve some cocoa into a soup bowl and put a few of the truffles at a time into this. Swirl the bowl round so that the truffles become beautifully rounded and evenly coated with cocoa. Leave in cool place until set firm.

CAKES

Rhoda's Teisen Lap

1 lb flour
4 oz lard
4 oz butter
2 teaspoons baking powder
7 oz sugar
8 oz currants
3 eggs
pinch of nutmeg
milk

Rub the fat into the flour and add the other dry ingredients. Beat the eggs well and add to the mixture. Then add enough milk to keep the mixture soft. Place in a shallow, greased and floured roasting dish and bake in a moderate oven (350°F) for 20 minutes and then lower the heat to 275°F for another 40 minutes.

Drinks

Mulled Wine

1 bottle of red wine
1 pint of water
Ribena (approx ½ a bottle, instead of sugar to sweeten)
juice of three lemons
a stick of cinnamon
10 cloves
1 teaspoon grated nutmeg
2 sliced oranges

Put all the ingredients together in a heavy saucepan, adding the Ribena to sweeten the taste, and slowly bring to the boil. Remove from the heat to allow the spices to infuse for ten minutes. Take out the stick of cinnamon to stop the flavour getting too strong and check for sweetness. Reheat, but do not boil, and ladle into pre-warmed mugs or glasses.

Tarragon Vodka

3-4 5" sprigs of fresh tarragon
1 bottle of vodka

Cut the tarragon at midsummer. All herbs are richer in flavour when there is the most sun. Use French tarragon not Russian tarragon, as Russian tarragon has no flavour. Add to vodka and leave for two or three months. Serve neat as cold as possible, i.e. from the freezer. It is especially good with caviar.

DRINKS

Bryan's Fruit Cup

2 pints diluted orange barley water
2 bottles of Guinness's Kaliber
sprig of mint
sliced cucumber, banana, or
a handful of strawberries or raspberries in season
a handful of borage flowers
ice

Put all the ingredients together in a water jug with the ice. Stir and drink. If it is thought that the barley water is too sweet use cartoned orange juice. Biddesden fruit cups are rarely the same twice.

When making the ice put a borage flower in each compartment of the ice tray so that when frozen each cube will have a delicate blue flower at its centre.

Sloe Gin

3 lbs sloes
30 oz sugar
5 pints gin or vodka

Pick the sloes after the first frost or if there is a competition for them between you and the birds, pick and place in the deep freeze overnight. Wash them before freezing. Put all the ingredients in a gallon jar and seal. Leave for at least 6 months, turning occasionally. Decant into manageable bottles and drink.

Elderflower Champagne

2 heads of elderflower
1½ lbs white sugar
2 tablespoons white wine vinegar
1 gallon water
juice and the rind of 1 lemon

Pick heads off flowers when in full bloom and put in a bucket with the lemon juice, sugar and vinegar and sliced lemon rind (no pith). Add cold water and leave for 24 hours. Strain into bottles and leave them for a minimum of a fortnight on their sides. The longer you can bear to leave them, the greater the flavour.

Orangeade

6 oranges (and a lemon)
3 pints of boiling water
2 or 3 lbs of sugar
1 oz citric acid
1 oz Epsom salts
½ oz tartaric acid

Finely grate the rind of the fruit and mix this with the boiling water, sugar, citric acid etc. Allow to cool a little and then add juice from the fruit. Makes about 4 bottles. To be diluted when drunk.

If my daughter's book seems good
For teaching artistry in food,
I must beg you, if you please,
To keep penultimate the cheese,
And so make perfect your repast
By keeping sweetness to the last.

BRYAN GUINNESS

Index

Apple Salad	42	Chocolate Cake	79
Avocado Mousse	22	Chocolate Mousse	64
		Chocolate Roll	71
Baked Alaska	60	Cold Tomato Soup	19
Baked Cabbage	42	Creamed Haddock	28
Blackcurrant Leaf Ice	74	Crumble	63
Borsch	17	Cumberland Sauce	34
Bramble Summer Pudding	70	Elderflower Champagne	92
Bread Sauce	34	Floating Island	70
Brown Bread Ice Cream	67	Fruit Cup	91
Brownies	78		
Brussels Sprouts	44	Georgian Pheasant	55
		Gianmarina's Pudding	73
Calf's Liver with Herbs and Mushrooms	48	Ginger Cake	82
		Ginger Cream	60
Carrots	40	Girdle Scones	80
Cheese Custards	23	Gooseberry Fool	61
Cheese Soufflé	23	Guinness Cake	83
Chicken Elizabeth	52	Guinness Christmas Pudding	74
Chicken Italian	50		
Chicken Liver Paté	28		
Chicken Maryland	54	Ham	49

Hedgehog	62	Roast Pork with Cider and	
Horseradish Sauce	36	Apple Jelly	52
Hot Chocolate Soufflé	66	Roast Potatoes	41
Kidney Beans with Ginger	44	Rowan Berry Jelly	37
Lemon Delight	62	Scotch Pancakes	84
		Shah of Persia	68
'Malt' Loaf	85	Shortbread Biscuits	82
Melting Moments	79	Sloe Gin	91
Mulled Wine	90	Soda Bread	83
Normandy Pheasant	56	Soufflé Glacé au Grand Marnier	64
Nutty Meringue	73	Spaghetti Sauce	35
Onions *à la Grècque*	41	Spinach Soup	16
Orangeade	92	Steamed Fish Starter	26
Orange Cake	85	Taramasalata	22
Pain d' Epices	80	Tarragon Vodka	90
Parsley Sauce	33	Teisen Lap	87
Pigeon Casserole	54	Toffee Pudding	63
Pink Sauce	38	Tomato Water Ice	27
Port Jelly	75	Venison Marinade	48
Potato and Basil	40	Vichyssoise	16
Potato Soup	18		
Poulet à la Grenouille	32	Watercress Soup	17
Prawn Cocktail	25	Welsh Cakes	78
Prawns	58	*Zabaglione*	67
Rhum Truffles 86			
Roast Duck	55